Railways of the
Isle of Wight
Marie Panter

Ryde Pier Head Station, 3 September 1965.

Stenlake Publishing Ltd

Interior of a smoking compartment, March 1960. The painting in the carriage appears to be of Salisbury Cathedral and not one of the island's beauty spots, a reminder that nearly all of the rolling stock was and still is second hand.

Acknowledgements

The publishers wish to thank the following people for their contributions to this book.

John Alsop, for the use of his picture collection on pages, IBC (both), 11 (upr), 12 (upr), 14 (both), 22 (upr), 24 (both), 25 (both), 26 (both), 27 (both), 29, 30 (upr), 31 (top), 32 (lwr), 33 (upr), 36 (lwr), 40 (lwr), 44 (both), 46, 47 (both), 53 (both), 59 (upr), 72 (upr), 76 (both), 78 (both), 80 (upr), 82, 83 (lwr), 84 (both), 85 (both), 91 (both), 92 and 94 (both).

Richard Casserley, for the use of his picture collection on pages, IFC (both), 4, 8 (both), 9 (both), 10 (both), 11 (lwr), 12 (lwr), 15 (both), 19 (upr), 31 (mid, bot), 32 (upr), 33 (lwr), 34, 36 (upr), 37 (upr), 41 (upr), 43 (lwr), 45 (lwr), 48 (both), 52 (both), 54 (both), 58 (both), 86 (upr), 90 and 95 (lwr).

The Heywood Collection, for the use of pictures on pages, FC, BC, 1, 2, 5 (both), 6, 16, 17 (both), 19 (lwr), 20, 22 (lwr), 23, 30 (lwr), 38, 40 (upr), 41 (lwr), 50, 54 (lwr), 55 (lwr), 56, 59 (lwr), 60, 61 (both), 62 (both), 64 (both), 65, 66 (both), 67, 68 (both), 69 (both), 70 (both), 72 (lwr), 73 (lwr), 74 (both), 75 (both), 77, 79 (both), 80 (lwr), 81 (lwr), 83 (upr), 86 (lwr), 87 (both) and 88.

Thanks to Lewis Hutton for the maps, writing the captions and a history of tunnel schemes.

Introduction

Located in the English Channel off the south coast of Great Britain, the Isle of Wight once had a whole network of railways measuring approximately 56 miles in total across the island, which is 24 miles long by 14 miles broad. There is little visible evidence of them now and the only lines remaining open and in use today are the Ryde to Shanklin line, known as the Island Line, and the Wootton to Smallbrook Junction line, more commonly known as The Isle of Wight Steam Railway.

Except for the first two miles from Ryde Pier Head, all the railways on the island were single track. They were run by three independent companies – the Isle of Wight Railway, the Isle of Wight Central Railway and the Freshwater, Yarmouth and Newport Railway. The first railway to open was the Isle of Wight Central Railway's Cowes and Newport line in 1862. This was built to connect Newport, the island's capital, to Cowes and the sea, and was only four and half miles in length. In 1900 the Isle of Wight Central Railway was also responsible for the final section of line to be opened on the island, from Ventnor Town to St Lawrence. The Isle of Wight Railway Company opened the island's second railway which ran from Ryde St John's Road to Shanklin (and later extended to Ventnor) on 23 August 1864, while the Freshwater, Yarmouth and Newport Railway opened on 10 September 1888.

Services on the island's railways were not fast. In 1914 the Ryde to Ventnor journey of twelve and a half miles took

between 37 and 45 minutes. There was a popular semi-fast train, 'The Tourist', which ran from Ventnor Town to Sandown, via Merstone and Newport, taking one hour and seventeen minutes. It then reversed and continued on to Freshwater. Fares were high on all the island's services, with third class fares only being introduced in 1914.

As with other railways in Britain, Grouping occurred on 1 January 1923 and the Isle of Wight Railway and the Isle of Wight Central Railway were amalgamated to form part of the Southern Railway group. The Freshwater, Yarmouth and Newport Railway remained independent until 1 August 1923, but it then too joined the Southern Railway. Nationalisation in 1948 saw the Southern Region of British Railways take responsibility for the island's railway network.

Closure of the island's railways began in the 1950s. The first line to close was the one from Ventnor West to Merstone in 1952. This was followed in 1953 by the Newport to Freshwater and Brading to Bembridge lines. 1956 saw the closure of the Sandown to Newport line and the final closures took place ten years later with services ending on the Ryde to Cowes and Shanklin to Ventnor lines. 1966 also marked the end of main line steam operation on the island. In 1967 the line from Ryde Pier Head to Shanklin underwent electrification and saw the introduction of ex-London Transport Underground rolling stock, which is still in use today.

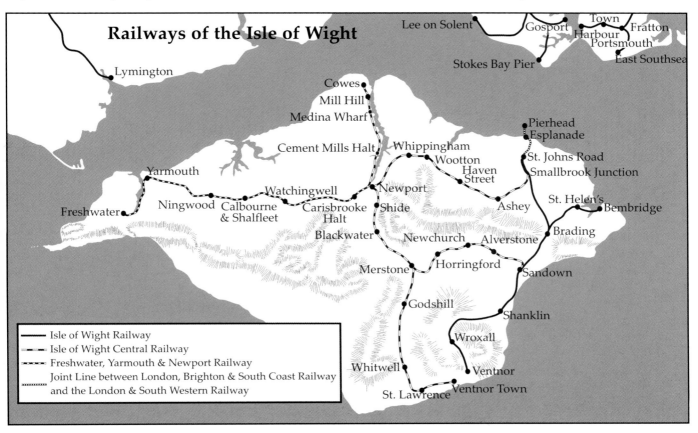

Railways of the Isle of Wight

Lymington
Lee on Solent
Gosport
Town Harbour
Portsmouth
Fratton
East Southsea
Stokes Bay Pier
Cowes
Mill Hill
Medina Wharf
Pierhead
Esplanade
Cement Mills Halt
Whippingham
St. Johns Road
Wootton
Smallbrook Junction
Haven Street
Yarmouth
Watchingwell
Newport
Ashey
St. Helen's
Ningwood
Calbourne & Shalfleet
Carisbrooke Halt
Shide
Bembridge
Freshwater
Blackwater
Newchurch
Alverstone
Brading
Merstone
Horringford
Sandown
Godshill
Shanklin
Wroxall
Whitwell
Ventnor
St. Lawrence
Ventnor Town

—— Isle of Wight Railway
–·–·– Isle of Wight Central Railway
-----· Freshwater, Yarmouth & Newport Railway
Joint Line between London, Brighton & South Coast Railway and the London & South Western Railway

The Tramway

Ryde Pier Gates to Pier Head

Passenger service	29 August 1864 – 27 January 1969
Distance	0.5 miles
Companies	Ryde Pier Company; Isle of Wight Railway; Southern Railway; British Railways

Ryde Pier Gates to The Castle

Passenger service	January 1870 – 5 April 1880
Distance	0.25 miles
Companies	Ryde Pier Company

The Castle to St John's Road

Passenger service	1 August 1871 – 5 April 1880
Distance	0.5 miles
Companies	Ryde Pier Company

At first the only way to travel the length of Ryde Pier was to walk. This was due to the timber decking being unsuitable for horsedrawn carriages, but the walk was long and particularly unpleasant in bad weather. In 1864 the decision was made to build another pier next to Ryde Pier and the two would connect at Ryde Pier Head: this second pier would carry the tramway.

Opened in three stages between 1864 and 1871, the tramway travelled from the pier head to Ryde esplanade. Pressure for better connection to Ryde Station at St John's Road saw the extension of the tramway to reach a temporary terminus at The Castle in January 1870. The extension from there into Ryde itself and then out to reach the railway station – even travelling through the middle of a building, Holywell House – opened in August 1871.

From opening the trams were horsedrawn. However, in 1885 the line was electrified, making Ryde Pier Tramway one of the first electric railways in the world (even earlier than the London Underground).

In 1927 petrol engine trams were introduced. These were converted to diesel in 1959 and remained in use until the closure of the tramway in 1969. Upon closure, the trams were removed and dismantled, although one can be seen in the museum in Newport.

The tramway before 1880 when the railway was built. The original pier is on the right and the tramway pier was built parallel to it. When the railway was built the tramway pier was sandwiched between the original pier and the railway pier.

Ryde Pier Head Station, the pier end terminus of the tramway, looking toward the Solent, 3 September 1965.

A petrol driven tram makes its way along the pier, March 1960. The pier head railway station and a steamer for Portsmouth are to the right.

On 12 July 1880 the tram line through Ryde to St John's Road closed and the pier gate once again became the terminus of the Ryde tramway. Ryde Pier Gates Station is seen here in March 1962.

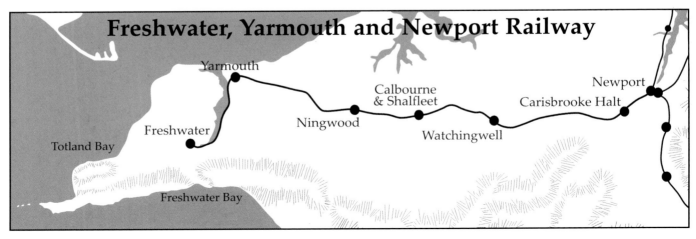

Freshwater, Yarmouth and Newport Railway

Yarmouth

Calbourne & Shalfleet

Newport

Carisbrooke Halt

Ningwood

Watchingwell

Freshwater

Totland Bay

Freshwater Bay

Freshwater, Yarmouth and Newport Railway

Passenger services	20 July 1889 – 21 September 1953
Distance	12 miles
Companies	Freshwater, Yarmouth and Newport Railway Company; Southern Railway; British Railways

Closed stations	*Opening date*	*Closing date*
Newport *	1 July 1913	1 August 1923
Carisbrooke Halt	20 July 1889	21 September 1953
Watchingwell Halt **	20 July 1889	21 September 1953
Calbourne & Shalfleet	20 July 1889	21 September 1953
Ningwood	20 July 1889	21 September 1953
Yarmouth	20 July 1889	21 September 1953
Freshwater	20 July 1889	21 September 1953

* Opened 1 July 1913, closed 1914, reopened January 1923 to 1 August 1923.
** Originally known as Watchingwell until 1948.

Authorised on 26 August 1880, construction of this railway was begun in 1886 by contractor William Jackson. Approximately 100 people were employed to build the railway, with the materials being brought across the Solent into a temporary dock at Yarmouth.

The line opened to goods traffic on 10 September 1888. Excursions ran during the year, but the line was not inspected for passenger traffic until May 1889. Upon inspection it was found that some remedial work was needed and once completed the line opened to passengers on 11 July that year. The Freshwater, Yarmouth and Newport Railway Company was responsible for the maintenance of the line, although rolling stock and staff were provided by the Isle of Wight Central Railway.

This arrangement continued on an uneasy basis for a number of years, including the bankruptcy of the FY&N Railway in 1896. Conflict intensified between the two companies and in 1913 the agreement ceased. This led to the FY&N purchasing its own rolling stock and engines, going bankrupt once again in the process. The company also built its own station just outside the main Newport station belonging to the Isle of Wight Central. This meant that transferring passengers had to walk between the two.

The FY&N operated in bankruptcy until 1923 when the line was taken over by the Southern Railway. The bankrupt nature of the company raised a dispute over the compensation for its compulsory purchase. This in turn delayed its grouping and resulted in the FY&N's Newport station being reopened for the duration of the dispute. Immediately after the takeover, the FY&N's Newport station closed and improvements were made to the line. Upon closure of the station all passenger trains worked into the bay platform of the Isle of Wight Central's Newport station. Also after the takeover the only named Isle of Wight train was put into operation, a through train from Ventnor to Freshwater known as 'The Tourist'.

Many of the seven stations on the line were situated some distance from the villages they were built to serve. Ningwood was a scattered village with very limited passenger potential. The station of Calbourne & Shalfleet did not attract much passenger traffic and was built midway between these two villages, with passengers from each having a mile's walk to the station. The station building was small with no separate accommodation for the passengers; they were required to use the station master's living room. Watchingwell was a private halt built for the use of Sir John Stephen Barrington Simion who owned the Swainston Estate. Family, friends, tenants and persons having business on the estate were also permitted to use the halt. The station at Carisbrooke was situated a half mile from the village and even further from Carisbrooke Castle (a popular tourist spot); there was no direct approach road to the station and in 1899 a private siding to Gunville Brickworks was added.

Yarmouth Station was at the back of the town, half a mile from the quay and landing point for the Lymington steamers, although luckily for passengers it was a level walk. There was a lengthy walk to Freshwater Station from Totland Bay in one direction and Freshwater Bay in the other. The station was located on marshland that had to be drained and filled before construction.

Locomotive No. W2 *Freshwater,* about to pass the site of FY&NR's Newport Station on 9 November 1928 with a train from Freshwater.

Watchingwell facing Newport, 3 September 1952.

Calbourne facing Newport, 20 June 1935.

Calbourne facing Freshwater, 3 September 1952.

Ningwood facing Freshwater, 3 September 1952.

Yarmouth facing Freshwater, 3 September 1952.

Freshwater Station, 1930.

Freshwater Station, 3 September 1952. The 3.25 Freshwater to Newport service is preparing to leave.

Freshwater Station, *c.* 1908. The horse buses are waiting to take tourists to Totland and Freshwater Bays from the arriving train.

Freshwater Station shortly before nationalisation in 1948.

Cowes to Newport Railway *

Passenger services	16 June 1862 – 21 February 1966	
Distance	4 ½ miles	
Companies	Cowes & Newport Railway; Isle of Wight Central Railway;	
	Southern Railway; British Railways	

Closed stations	*Opening date*	*Closing date*
Cowes	16 June 1862	21 February 1966
Mill Hill	16 June 1862	21 February 1966
Medina Wharf Halt	1890s	21 February 1966
Cement Mills Halt	1890s	21 February 1966
Newport	16 June 1862	21 February 1966

Authorised on 8 August 1859 and opened three years later, the Cowes & Newport Railway was the first line on the island and was built to connect Newport, the island's capital, to Cowes and the sea. Classed as a 'Little Railway', it ran along the route of the Medina river and was only four and a half miles in length. Also, it had only two locomotives and five season ticket holders.

There was a quiet opening, with only half a dozen passengers travelling on the first train at 8.15 a.m. on 16 June 1862. One of the first passengers was Michael Ratsey of the famous Cowes sail firm; he had also cut the first sod of the railway on 16 October 1859.

Although it was authorised, a tramway from Cowes Station to the town's pier was never constructed due to opposition from the Cowes local board and, although close to the sea, the station at Cowes did not permit a direct interchange with the Southampton steamers which is what the tramway was intended to provide.

The station at Cowes was located on a sloping site and was a brick and stone two-storey building which looked fairly impressive to passengers arriving up the hill from Fountain Quay. The accommodation on the lower level of the station building was used as offices by the Cowes & Newport Railway and Joint Committee, although the rooms were later let out when larger company premises were built at Newport. Next to the station building was a flight of wooden stairs leading up to the platform, booking office and waiting room. The station was well known for its floral displays and was busy enough to boast a W.H. Smith's bookstall during the tourist season.

The station at Mill Hill was situated in a cramped location between the railway and Newport Road. The station was further hindered by the sharp right-hand curve of the line and also by being several feet below road level. In 1914 electric lighting was installed there.

Medina Wharf was the principal entry into the island for coal and heavy goods (including, when required, locomotives and coaches). The wharf itself was served by a short spur from the main railway. Workers at the wharf had a halt provided on the main line. The opening date of the Medina Wharf Halt is uncertain as is the date for the Cement Mills Halt. which provided a similar service for workers at the West Medina Cement Works of the Francis Company. Neither halt was mentioned on any timetable, but operated as request stops.

Newport was the line's terminus. The Cowes & Newport Railway's Newport station was the first of the town's two stations to be built and the only one to survive both the Grouping and nationalisation of the island's railways.

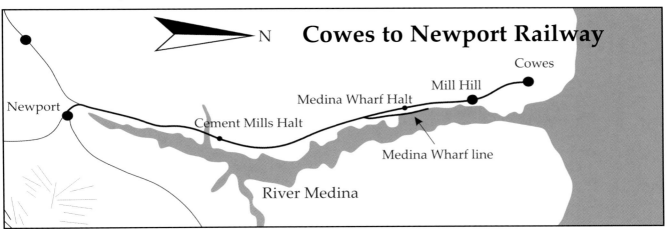

Isle of Wight Central Railway No. 10, pulling out of Cowes, *c.* 1905. The locomotive was built in 1874 by the London, Brighton and South Coast Railway and entered service with them as No. 69, *Peckham.* In April 1900 it was bought by the island company.

IWCR No. 12 arrived on the island in 1903; it was originally London, Brighton and South Coast Railway's No. 84 *Crowborough,* built in 1880. The locomotive is seen here leaving Cowes Station with a train for Sandown.

Cowes Station, 27 June 1953. Enough is visible of the bus on the right to suggest it was going to Fountain Quay to meet the ferry.

The dead end at Cowes Station, 27 June 1953.

Locomotive No. W22 *Brading* at Cowes Station, 5 September 1965. Built in 1892, *Brading* was originally London and South Western Railway No. 215. It had worked on the mainland until its transfer to the island by the Southern Railway in 1924.

On 17 November 1964 No. W14 *Fishbourne* arrives at Cowes from Ryde Pier Head. The locomotive was built in 1889 by the London and South Western Railway and was transferred to the Isle of Wight in May 1936.

A little later on the 17 November 1964, No. W14 runs around to the back of the carriages so that the train can leave tender first for Ryde.

Train leaving bunker first from Cowes, 27 June 1953. No. W25 *Godshill* was, like the majority of the locomotives, old London and South Western Railway stock. Built in 1890, she came to the island in 1925 and was retired in December 1962.

No. W22 approaches a set of carriages in preparation of taking a train to Ryde at Cowes Station, 5 September 1965.

A view of Cowes Station on 17 November 1964, taken from the roadbridge visible in the background of the lower photograph on page 19. T. Grange and Son's coal yard is tucked neatly behind the signal box on the left.

Mill Hill Station. The photograph is undated but the Nestlé Swiss Milk advertisments suggest an Edwardian date.

A train pulled by No. W17 *Seaview* at Mill Hill Station, September 1965. The engine was formerly London and South Western Railway No. 208 and had been built in 1891. It was moved to the island in May 1930.

Mill Hill Station, 17 November 1964,

A series of photographs taken on one day during the construction on the new Medina Wharf in the early 1930s. The new quay was completed by 1933 and replaced the old railway pier that the SS *Camberway* can be seen lying alongside. The wharf was the main point of entry for coal and other bulk goods to and from the island.

The *Camberway* was owned by the Sunderland Steam Shipping Co. between 1931 and 1932, which limits the date of the photographs to that period. She was built in 1919 in Barcelona and sailed as an Estonian registered vessel for most of the 1920s. During the 1930s she had a number of owners and names, including her period as the *Camberway,* before once again being registered as an Estonian vessel in 1937. During the Second World War the ship was requisitioned by the American War Shipping Administration and turned over to the US Navy in 1942, serving the rest of the war as a salvage ship. After the war she became a Panamanian registered vessel and resumed merchant service until 1955.

Newport Motive Power Depot (MPD) sometime before 1948. In the shed itself can be seen No. W25 *Godshill,* while No. W26 *Whitwell* sits in the middle and No. W11 *Newport* is on the right. *Newport* was built by the London, Brighton and South Coast Railway in 1878 and entered their service as No. 40 *Brighton.* In 1902 she was bought by the Isle of Wight Central Railway for £600 and moved to the island. After Grouping she worked until removed from service in 1946, was returned to the mainland and reconditioned in 1947 by the Southern Railway. The engine continued to work on the mainland until removed from service in 1963.

In earlier days No. W11 *Newport* was owned by the Isle of Wight Central Railway and was their No. 11 (without the name). She is seen here *c.* 1913 at Newport Station with a train that is going to Cowes tender first.

IWCR No. 7 arrives at Newport Station with a train that it has pulled bunker first. No. 7 was built by Beyer, Peacock of Gorton near Manchester for the Midland and South Western Junction Railway in 1882 and became their No. 6. The M&SWJR was a small railway company that connected the Midland Railway's lines at Cheltenham to those of the London and South Western at Andover. The locomotive was sold and arrived on the island in December 1906. She survived the Grouping of 1923 by a couple of years, the Southern Railway withdrawing her from service in April 1925.

Newport Station, *c.* 1920.

Sandown to Newport

Passenger services	1 June 1879 – 6 February 1956
Distance	9 miles
Companies	Isle of Wight (Newport Junction) Railway; Isle of Wight Central Railway; Southern Railway; British Railways

Stations	*Opening date*	*Closing date*
Sandown *	23 August 1864	still open
Alverstone	1 February 1875	6 February 1956
Newchurch	1 February 1875	6 February 1956
Horringford	1 February 1875	6 February 1956
Merstone **	1 February 1875	6 February 1956
Blackwater (IoW) ***	1 February 1875	6 February 1956
Shide	1 February 1894	6 February 1956
Newport Pan Lane	6 October 1875	1 June 1879

* Station on Isle of Wight Railway.
** The first Merstone Station was replaced on 20 July 1895 by Merstone Junction Station, which was on the opposite side of the level crossing. This station was renamed Merstone on 1 October 1911.
*** Originally named Blackwater (IoWC) until 9 July 1923.

Although authorisation for the Sandown to Newport line as a whole was received on 31 July 1868, the line actually opened in three sections between 1875 and 1879: Sandown to Shide on 1 February 1875, Shide to Pan Lane on 6 October 1875, and Pan Lane to Newport on 1 June 1879. The line ran along the Yar Valley.

Three quarters of a mile short of Sandown, there was a 190-feet siding built in 1905 to serve the Isle of Wight Waterworks Company. From this point the line ascended steeply for approximately half a mile (the steepest gradient on the Isle of Wight Central Railway) from the valley of the Easter Yar before entering Sandown.

Alverstone had no great residential population, other than the Webster family's tenants. The site of the station was literally surrounded by streams, the main line crossing one of them. Newchurch Station was located half a mile downhill from the village itself.

Horringford was intended to be the first terminus of the line. Being located a mile from Arreton village, like other stations on the line it lost most of its passenger traffic to the omnibus. From here there was a siding from which a spur ran half a mile to a gravel pit.

From 6 October 1875 to 1 June 1879 Newport Pan Lane was the temporary line terminus. The station had a 180-feet platform, a booking shed and a signal box. There was originally a run-round loop, but this was removed when the line into Newport opened. The line from Newport Pan Lane to Shide was mostly level, although there were bridges going across streams: Shide Water Bridge, Shide Bridge and Shide Brick Bridge.

Shide Station was located at the southern extremity of Newport. There was a single platform and a red-brick single-storey booking office. There had been a run-round loop to the north of the platform, but this was removed when the line to Newport Pan Lane opened. Electric lighting was installed at Shide in 1913 and there was a connection from the station to a chalk pit and flour mill.

Between Shide and Blackwater, a little way from the railway was a rope-worked incline to Ruffin Blake's gravel pit – this was one of the many industrial tramways on the island.

Upon entry into Newport the railway passed over a level crossing and then on to the 700-feet, 18-arch brick-built Newport Viaduct which curved approximately 90 degrees around the edge of the town. There were seven arches followed by a 97-feet steel lattice girder bridge, then a bridge crossing both a road and the river, a further three arches, and then a 24-feet wrought iron crossing over the river before the final eight arches.

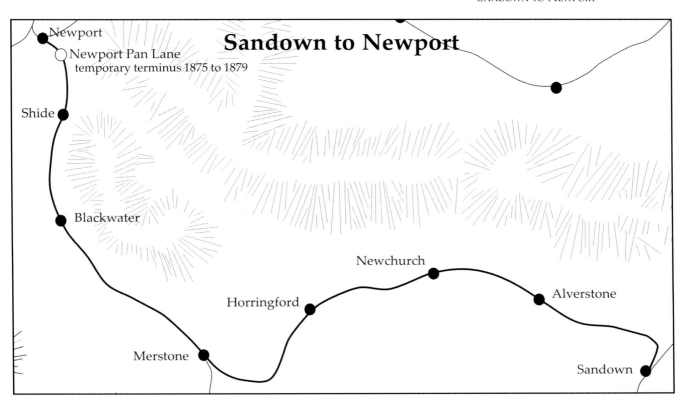

Sandown to Newport

Newport
Newport Pan Lane
temporary terminus 1875 to 1879
Shide
Blackwater
Newchurch
Alverstone
Horringford
Merstone
Sandown

Isle of Wight Central Railway No. 4 *Cowes* leaves Sandown Station with a train for Newport, *c.* 1913. No. 4 was a survivor from the Ryde and Newport Railway Company. It was built in Gorton, near Manchester, by Beyer, Peacock in 1876, so was unusual because it had been built for the island company. It was withdrawn from service in September 1925 by the Southern Railway.

IWC No. 11 approaches Sandown Station with a train from Newport, *c.* 1913.

By the time of this photograph, taken on 1 April 1960, the track had been lifted. However, the curve of the trackbed of the line from Sandown to Newport is conspicuous. The four locomotives sitting on the siding are in winter storage.

Alverston Station. *c.* 1910.

Alverstone Station, 27 June 1953.

Alverstone Station from the road, 27 June 1953.

Newchurch Station, 27 June 1953.

Horringford Station, June 1950.

Merstone Station in the 1930s.

Merstone Station, facing Newport, 27 June 1953.

Merstone Station, looking south at the point where the line divided left to Sandown and right toward Ventnor West. No. W27 *Merstone* is pulling the 3.56 Cowes – Sandown service. No. W35 *Freshwater* is heading to Ventnor West with the 4.25 Newport – Ventnor West service. *Freshwater* arrived in April 1949 and worked for seventeen years before being withdrawn in October 1966.

Blackwater Station, facing Newport, 27 June 1953.

Shide Station, facing Newport, 27 June 1953

Shide Station, looking south, 1930

A view of Newport from a train window looking south along the disused line to Sandown and Ventnor West, March 1960.

Newport, March 1960, looking along the line to Merstone.

Newport Station and yard, *c.* 1930.

No. W25 *Godshill* setting out for Cowes from Newport Station, 3 September 1952. No. W17 *Seaview* stands to the right. She spent 36 years working the island's railways from her arrival in 1930 until withdrawal from service in December 1966.

The eastern end of the platform at Newport Station, November 1964. No. W33 *Bembridge* waits with a train for Ryde, its path blocked by the engine on the retractable bridge over the River Medina. The bridge was pulled back by muscle power into a recess below track level on the station side of the viaduct. In the background, between the two locomotives, the signal post that once controlled the junction of the lines to Ryde and Sandown/Ventnor West can be seen.

Ventnor Town to Merstone

Passenger services	26 July 1897 – 15 September 1952
Distance	6.75 miles
Companies	Newport, Godshill & St Lawrence Railway;
	Isle of Wight Central Railway;
	Southern Railway; British Railways

Closed Stations	*Opening date*	*Closing date*
Ventnor Town *	1 June 1900	15 September 1952
St Lawrence Halt for Blackgang **	26 July 1897	15 September 1952
Whitwell Halt ***	26 July 1897	15 September 1952
Godshill Halt for Sandford †	20 July 1897	15 September 1952

* Originally named Ventnor Town until renamed Ventnor West on 9 July 1923.
** Originally named Ventnor (St Lawrence) until renamed St Lawrence in July 1900.
Renamed again in 1927.
*** Originally named Whitwell until 1 July 1941.
† Originally named Godshill until 1928.

Opened in two sections, this line connected Merstone to St Lawrence and eventually Ventnor Town. The first section to open was between Merstone and St Lawrence on 26 July 1897, a distance of five and a half miles with four stations. The second section, which had no stations, was opened on 1 June 1900.

Despite being in a quiet location, Merstone had generous facilities for passengers, including a lengthy canopy over the platform to protect them while they were changing trains. The subway was rarely used due to persistent flooding and the crossing loop was the only one on the island that crossed two running lines.

Godshill Station was situated in the shadow of Bleak Down. There was a two-storey station master's house with single-storey additions for the booking office and other facilities. It was a substantial building and as with those at Whitwell and St Lawrence, the ground floor level was red brick, whereas the upper storey was decorated with strips of plain concrete on roughcast to give a half timbered effect.

The line between Godshill and Whitwell was carried partly on a long straight embankment, which was the largest on the island. The station at Whitwell was located on a hill at the back of the village and it also served Niton, Blackgang and Chale. There was a crossing loop here for the Merstone to Ventnor line, although it was rarely used and during Russell Wilhott's time in office it was secured out of use.

The major engineering structure on the line was High Hat Tunnel. Depending on which wall was measured, the tunnel was either 619 or 625 yards, 2 feet in length and had a height of 15 feet 4 inches from the rails to the crown of the arch. Within the tunnel the railway took an almost 90 degrees curve and fell steeply and, upon leaving it, passengers were given a breathtaking view of the undercliff as the line fell and curved to the left. St Lawrence Halt was situated on a narrow site where the road from the village crossed the railway (on a stone-faced road bridge).

The second section to open continued the line on from St Lawrence to Ventnor Town (the second of Ventnor's stations) and this station became the terminus of the line. It was built one mile to the west of the town in the grounds of Steephill Castle; the difficult negotiations with the Steephill Estate were solved when six acres of land were purchased for the sum of £5,000. The completed line from Merstone officially opened on 1 June 1900 and was to be the final stretch of railway to be built on the island. It is said that had the most attractive scenery of any of the island's railways.

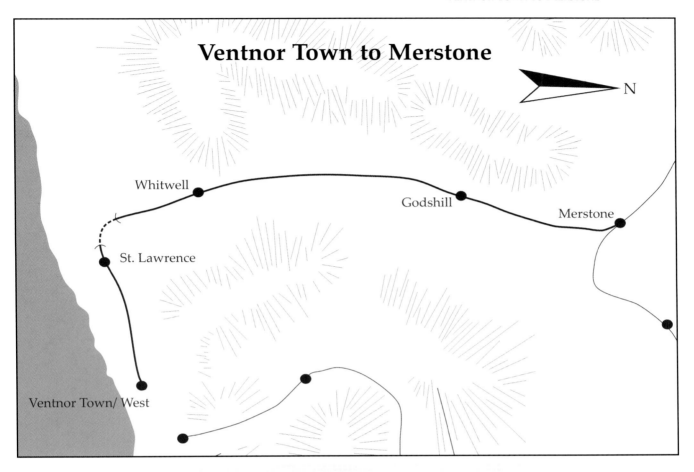

Ventnor West, facing the dead end, 27 June 1953.

Ventnor West, looking towards the dead end, 1930.

Ventnor West in 1934, looking towards Merstone.

Ventnor West, with No. W35 *Freshwater* approaching, June 1953.

St Lawrence Station, looking towards Ventnor, 1930.

The line to Ventnor Town (West) was famed for its stunning coastal scenery, a view afforded to the passengers of this train being drawn by No. 9 of the Isle of Wight Central Railway towards Merstone. No. 9, formerly of the London, Brighton and South Coast Railway (their No. 75 *Blackwall*), was built in 1872. It arrived on the island in March 1899 and was withdrawn from service by the Southern Railway in April 1927.

A train pulled by No. 10 of the IWCR makes its way towards Ventnor Town.

Whitwell Station, facing Merstone, 9 November 1928.

Godshill Station, 3 May 1952.

Newport to Ryde St John's Road

Passenger services		20 December 1875 – 21 February 1966
Distance		10 miles
Companies		Ryde and Newport Railway;
		Isle of Wight Central Railway;
		Southern Railway; British Railways

Closed station	*Opening date*	*Closing date*
Newport	16 June 1862	21 February 1966
Whippingham	20 December 1875	21 September 1953
Wootton *	20 December 1875	21 September 1953
Havenstreet **	20 December 1875	21 February 1966
Ashey *	20 December 1875	21 February 1966

* Reopened on the Isle of Wight Steam Railway on 31 May 1971. Wootton was resited in 1987.
** Originally named Haven Street until 9 June 1958; reopened on the Isle of Wight Steam Railway on 31 May 1971.

At ten miles in length and connecting Newport to Ryde, this line was one of the longest on the island. It was authorised on 25 July 1872 and opened on 20 December 1875. Just after Newport Station the lines to Ryde and Sandown separated. The Ryde line crossed the Medina Valley on a retractable bridge and a brick viaduct, then entered the Newport Tunnel which measured some 73 yards in length.

The first station out of Newport was Whippingham. Often described as 'Whippingham for Osborne', the station was a little over two miles from Osborne House and one and a half miles from the hamlet of Whippingham. The station received little traffic and was originally a private station for the royal residence.

Wootton was occasionally referred to as 'Wootton for Woodside'. The station was situated at the summit of the line, approximately one mile south of the village and in a steep cutting. A substantial three-arch brick bridge spanned the cutting.

In 1886 a siding was constructed at Havenstreet, around the same time as a gas works was built opposite the station. Although the gas works closed in 1920 the siding remained in use for goods traffic. The original station was replaced in 1926.

Styled as 'Ashey for Nunwell', the station was located nowhere near any centre of population and therefore generated very little traffic. For many years the only crossing loop on the line was located at Ashey. From here there was a connection to a quarry which was high up under the lee of Ashey Down, approximately half a mile from the station. Ashey Station eventually came to life after the opening of a nearby racecourse in April 1882 and the Isle of Wight Railway and the Isle of Wight Central Railway worked special trains carrying upwards of 3,000 passengers per day, all going to the course. From here the line travelled under Deacons Lane Bridge where in 1899 there was a halt built to serve a temporary territorial army camp. The final curve of the line took it past Smallbrook Farm and alongside the Isle of Wight Railway line from Ventnor to Ryde St John's Road.

In 1971 Ashey, Wootton and Havenstreet stations reopened as part of the Isle of Wight Steam Railway. In 1991 a station was constructed and opened at Smallbrook Junction where the Isle of Wight Steam Railway meets the Island Line from Ryde to Shanklin; the only means of access to this station is by train.

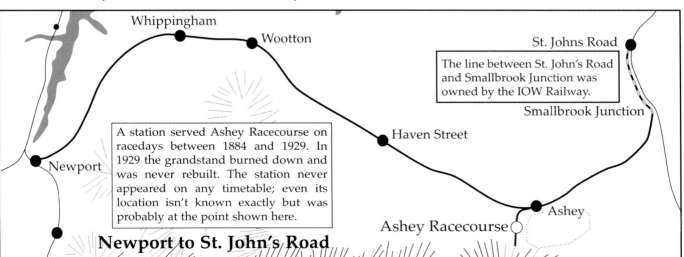

Newport Station in November 1964, looking east from the end of the platform, where the long viaduct curves round to carry the line to Ryde. At the end of that viaduct closest to the camera is the bridge that crossed the River Medina in three spans, the nearest span contained the retractable section. The dark line on the bridge deck marks the far end of its telescopic extent. Originally there were two parallel retractable sections of the same span to the bridge, but by the time of this photograph only one remains.

Whippingham Station, 27 June 1953. The upper photograph looks east towards Ryde and the lower one to Newport.

Wooton Station, 26 August 1953. The view along the platform looks towards Ryde and the ticketing office built neatly into one of the arches of the road viaduct (see below).

Haven Street Station, 14 May 1964, facing Newport. No. W30 *Shorwell* is taking a train to Ryde.

No. W18 *Ningwood* at Haven Street with a train for Newport, 3 September 1965

Haven Street Station, looking towards Ryde, 3 September 1965

Ashey Station, 2 September 1952.

A train drawn by No. W31 *Chale* passes the old Ashey Station buildings on its way to Ryde, 31 August 1965. Subsidence caused by the clay soils necessitated the abandonment of the old station building and lifting of the platform in the 1950s. Consequently the station was resited and became an unmanned halt. This photograph is taken from the end of the new platform.

Both pictures on this page show St John's Road Station, the upper photograph taken in the 1930s and the lower one in September 1965. To the left of the signal box in the 1930s photograph is the engine shed where No. W18 *Ningwood* sits under cover. In the lower picture *Ningwood* features again, at the head of a train and looking a little worn. To the right of the station, in both photographs, are the works where engines were serviced and conditioned.

These three photographs show Haven Street Station in September 1985. After closure of the line to Newport in 1966, it lay in disuse until 1971 when the Isle of Wight Steam Railway reopened the section between Ashey and Wooton as a tourist attraction.

In 1985 there were no services to Wooton. All that existed at that time was this loop so that engines could be uncoupled from a train then run around the carriages to the other end to pull the train back to Haven Street. The remains of the old Wooton platform can be seen to the right of the line in this photograph. In 1987 a resited station was created by extending the disused platform, allowing passengers to once again depart a train at Wooton.

Smallbrook Junction, September 1965, a time when there was no station whatsoever at Smallbrook. On 20 July 1991 the Isle of Wight Steam Railway opened a station here to allow interchange between their line and the Island Line. The new station is unusual because there are no roads to it, and its only purpose is to serve as an interchange between the two lines. As a result it is only served when the steam railway is running trains.

Ryde Pier Head to Shanklin – the 'Island Line'

Passenger services	23 August 1864 – Present
Distance	8.5 miles
Companies	Isle of Wight Railway;
	Southern Railway;
	British Railways;
	Island Line Franchise;
	South Western Franchise

Station	Opening date	Closing date
Ryde Pier Head	12 July 1880	Still open
Ryde Esplanade	5 April 1880	Still open
Ryde St John's Road *	23 August 1864	Still open
Smallbrook Junction	20 July 1991	Still open
Brading	23 August 1864	Still open
Sandown	23 August 1864	Still open
Lake	11 May 1987	Still open
Shanklin	23 August 1864	Still open

* Opened as Ryde 23 August 1864; renamed Ryde St John's Road 5 April 1880.

Authorised on 23 July 1860, the line from Ryde St John's Road to Shanklin was the first to be opened by the Isle of Wight Railway Company. The line opened on 23 August 1864 and has always been considered the island's main line. Originally built as single track throughout, there were passing loops at Brading, Sandown and Shanklin stations. In 1880 the London and South Western Railway and the London, Brighton and South Coast Railway opened a jointly owned, double tracked extension of the line from Ryde to St John's Road to Ryde Pier Head. This included the construction of a new tunnel and a third pier to enable the line to reach the pier head and the connecting ferry services to the mainland.

In 1926 cross-over rails and a signal box were installed at Smallbrook Junction to enable the extension of the double track from Ryde St John's Road. The signal box was only used during the summer when the traffic levels were high. In the winter the two lines reverted back to independent single track operation. In 1927 the passing loops at Brading and Sandown were connected to form a second section of double track.

On 17 September 1966 steam trains were withdrawn from Ryde Pier and by 31 December, the whole line. The line was closed during the winter of 1966/67 to allow for electrification works to be carried out. During this time the track bed in Ryde Tunnel was raised to reduce flooding and decrease gradients. The station at Ryde Pier Head was rebuilt and Ryde Esplanade Station was substantially modified. The line ripened to the public in March 1967. Due to the work carried out in the tunnel, the ceiling was now 10 feet too low for standard national rail vehicles to clear, so since the electrification of the line old London Underground stock has been used. The initial trains were Class 485 and Class 486 units, which dated from 1923. By 1992 these had been replaced by newly refurbished Class 483 units built in 1938.

While the line was under the control of British Railways, two new stations were opened: Lake Station in 1987 and Smallbrook Junction in 1995, opened with the co-operation of the Isle of Wight Steam Railway. There is no public access to Smallbrook Junction. It was built to provide a connection between the Island Line and the Isle of Wight Steam Railway. The station is only served on days when the steam railway is in operation. By the early 1980s Brading was one of the last stations within British Railways to retain gas lighting. In 1985 this was converted from gas to fluorescent bulbs, although the original fittings remained. A few of these still survive today. During the late 1980s the double track between Sandown and Brading, along with the Brading passing loop, was removed. It was also at this time that the passenger service was branded as "Island Line" for the first time, the name and logo being included on the new Class 483 train livery. However the official rebranding did not happen until 1994.

Following the privatisation of British Rail, the rights to run services on the line were put out to tender as a franchise. On the national rail network the franchise was unique, as it also required the successful bidder to maintain the line in addition to the stations and trains. Stagecoach Group won the bid and from October 1996 operated passenger services under the name "Island Line".

In March 2006 the line was designated by the Department of Transport as a "Community Railway" (a local railway which is specially supported by local organisations). The following February the Island Line franchise merged with the South Western franchise on the mainland. Stagecoach Group was again the successful bidder for the expanded franchise and now operates the Island Line under their South West Trains subsidiary. The "Island Line" name has been retained, styled as "Island Line Trains" and is promoted as a separate division on the South West Trains website.

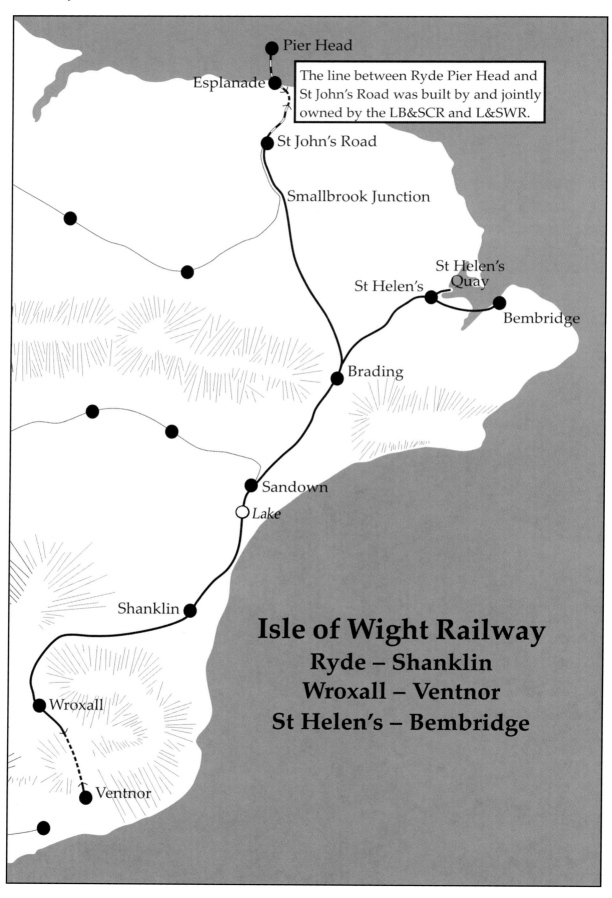

Pier Head

Esplanade

The line between Ryde Pier Head and St John's Road was built by and jointly owned by the LB&SCR and L&SWR.

St John's Road

Smallbrook Junction

St Helen's Quay

St Helen's

Bembridge

Brading

Sandown

Lake

Shanklin

Wroxall

Ventnor

Isle of Wight Railway
Ryde – Shanklin
Wroxall – Ventnor
St Helen's – Bembridge

MV *Shanklin* (seen above in March 1960) was the last of three sister ships built for the Portsmouth – Ryde ferry service. The ships were built by Denny & Brothers of Dumbarton in Scotland and launched in 1951, replacing two paddle steamers that had been lost after striking mines during the Second World War. Initially the three were very successful but latterly suffered as a result of the increasing use of car ferries. *Shanklin* was the least reliable and was relegated to relief use. In 1980 *Shanklin* was sold to the Paddle Steamer Preservation Society who renamed her *Prince Ivanhoe*. However, her time with the society was cut short when in August 1981 she hit an uncharted object off Port Enyon beach in South Wales that opened up a considerable gash in her hull. Fortunately, the ship's captain was able to beach the ship and all the passengers made it to shore safely. *Prince Ivanhoe*, however, was declared a loss and scrapped.

The disused Edwardian steamer indicator at Ryde Pier Head, March 1962. The destinations were Swanage, Eastbourne, Weymouth, Brighton, Bournemouth, Round the Island, Cowes Direct, Southampton and Southsea Clarence Pier.

PS *Ryde* (seen here in September 1965) and her sister ship the PS *Sandown* were commissioned by the Southern Railway as passenger ferries between the island and the mainland. The *Ryde* was launched by Denny & Brothers of Dumbarton in 1937 and cost £46,000. During the Second World War she worked initially as a minesweeper and latterly as an anti aircraft vessel. After the war she returned to her work as a ferry and was used for charter trips until 1969 when she was retired in favour of more modern motor vessels. After retiral she was bought, renamed the *Ryde Queen,* and turned into a nightclub at Binfield Marina near Newport. The nightclub closed in the late 1980s and the *Ryde* has lain rotting ever since. By 2013 the bridge and other parts of the ship had collapsed and the *Ryde*, despite the effort of enthusiasts to save her, looks set to be scrapped.

No. W33 *Bembridge* waits with a train at Ryde Pier Head Station, September 1965. In the upper photograph we are looking at the end of the pier and in the lower one towards Ryde and the esplanade.

In September 1966 steam traction was withdrawn from the pier and in December over the entire line to Shanklin. The line then closed until 20 March 1967 to allow the route to be electrified. During that period the Pier Head Station was greatly modified (compare with the pictures on the previous page). The platforms were widened, the awning marks their former edge, and the number of lines into the station was reduced. As a result of regrading of the line, within the Ryde Tunnel the head room was reduced and the only practical rolling stock was former London Underground trains. Two classes of train were established on the line, Class 485, a four car set, and Class 486, a three car set. In the photograph above, from September 1985, a Class 485 waits to take a train down the line. The panorama below looks towards Ryde, also in September 1985.

On 27 January 1969 the pier tramway closed. This photograph, taken across the former tram pier in October 1976, shows its skeletal form stretching towards Ryde after the rails were removed.

Photographs of Ryde Esplanade Station, both taken during September 1965. The upper one looks towards the pier head and a tram can be seen on the left hand side. The lower photograph looks toward Ryde.

The view towards St John's Road Station from the platform end of Ryde Esplanade Station, November 1964.

The 11.25 Ryde (Pier Head) – Ventnor service near St John's Road, 31 March 1962.

Ryde St John's Road Station in the 1930s, looking south.

The engine works at St John's Road half hidden in the steam from No. W21 *Sandown* taking the 4.18 Ryde Pier Head – Cowes service in March 1962.

No. W27 *Merstone* with a coal train passing the St John's Road signal box, September 1965.

A series of four photographs taken in March 1962 of the Motive Power Depot at St John's Road. In the photograph above and in the one to the right No. W20 *Shanklin* is seen directly in front of the entrance, gently steaming. The locomotive in the photograph below is No. W29 *Alverstone*.

The interior of the depot. No. W30 *Shorwell*, No. W36 *Carisbrook* and an unknown locomotive with a sign saying that it was 'NOT TO BE MOVED' are on the left; No. W26 *Whitwell* is on the right.

An unknown locomotive of the Isle of Wight Railway arrives at Brading Station in 1904, .

Brading Station looking in the opposite direction (north), in the early 1900s as Isle of Wight Railway locomotive *Sandown* arrives with a train. *Sandown* was one of the original three locomotives owned by the company and was built by Beyer, Peacock in 1864. She must have been fairly worn out by the time of the Grouping as the Southern Railway withdrew her in September 1923 after only nine months in their service and thus never received one of the W prefixes that formed their numbering system. Her name survived on locomotive No. W21 which arrived on the island the following year. On the right of the island platform a string of carriages can be seen, presumably waiting to take passengers along the branch line to Bembridge.

Looking south from Brading Station, September 1965, as an unknown locomotive heads off towards Ventnor.

A dramatic photograph looking south at Sandown Station, *c.* 1904, where a man seems determined to make the train at the opposite platform. After his jump he would have had to cross the duckboards provided and use the steps recessed in the platform wall to reach the level of the waiting train. Let's hope he caught it.

As a junction between the Isle of Wight Central Railway and Isle of Wight Railway networks, Sandown, seen here looking north in 1934, was an important station on the island. The leftmost platform belonged to the Isle of Wight Central and served the trains for Merstone and Newport. Curiously, perhaps because the station served both companies, no bridge between the platforms was provided, which must have encouraged the actions of the passenger in the upper picture.

A bunker first train for Ryde arrives at Sandown, September 1965.

A Class 485 four car set at Sandown, October 1976.

An unknown locomotive of the Isle of Wight Railway at Shanklin *c.* 1905. Its nameplate is very short, so it is probably *Ryde*, one of the first three ordered by the IOWR. *Ryde* arrived on the island in June 1864 and lasted until July 1932, receiving the number W13 at the Grouping of 1923.

No. W32 *Bonchurch* arrives at Shanklin Station with a train for Ventnor, April 1960.

A Class 486 three car set at Shanklin Station, September 1985. The line beyond here had been closed in 1966.

Shanklin to Ventnor

Passenger services	10 September 1866 – 18 April 1966
Distance	4 miles
Companies	Isle of Wight Railway; Southern Railway; British Railways

Closed Stations	*Opening date*	*Closing date*
Wroxall	10 September 1866	18 April 1966
Ventnor	10 September 1866	18 April 1966

For the construction of the line from Shanklin to Ventnor, authorised in 23 July 1860, there was a steep gradient to be constructed over Apse Bank. The bank is named after the nearby Apse Manor and was generally considered to be the stretch from Shanklin to Wroxall, although the long climb actually started before Shanklin and did not end until the Ventnor Tunnel. The climb up the bank required the best performance from both the locomotive and the crew, but the return trip was more relaxed – there are even rumours of the trains stopping to allow the passengers to carry out a bit of illicit mushroom picking!

The main problem with the construction of the line was the cutting of the 1,312 yard long tunnel through St Boniface Down. It was this tunnel which brought the line into Ventnor from the north. Ventnor Station itself was built 294 feet above sea level; this meant access from the town was up a steep hill. This caused problems for people on foot and also for horsedrawn carriages and cabs.

The line opened on 10 September 1866 and from the start it was well used and especially so when the Royal National Hospital for Chest Diseases was built in Ventnor. Patients came from all over the country and were able to travel easily and in comfort from Ryde direct to Ventnor. In 1891 non-stop trains known as 'Invalid Specials' were introduced by the railway company. They were discontinued in 1908.

The line was by no means straightforward; there was the three-quarter mile tunnel, five over bridges and seven under bridges, one of which was Three Arch Bridge, a considerable brick-faced structure which was certainly too lavish for the footpath it carried. Two arches measured 25 feet and the third measured 27 feet.

Wroxall was the only intermediate station. The line ran along the back of the village on a shelf cut into the hillside. The station itself was located a short way to the south of Wroxall Bridge, a three-arch road over bridge which led to Cook's Castle, an eighteenth-century romantic ruin. The station had no loading bank, which meant that there was no provision for loading and unloading horses, carriages, furniture vans, etc.

Wroxall from the road bridge, 1930.

An exchange of tickets at Wroxall Station for the line north to Ryde, September 1965.

An early view of Ventnor Station. The exact date is uncertain but it was probably taken during the 1870s as the signboards of the station make reference to using the tram to travel from Ryde Station to the pier head.

A view of Ventnor Station in the 1890s, looking towards to the tunnel. The limitations of the original station had become apparent, especially the restricted space available. The simple solution was to make the site bigger by quarrying the chalk of the Down away to make more room.

Ryde emerges from the tunnel at Ventnor with a train.

Ventnor Station from above the turntable *c.* 1910. A substantial remodeling of the station has taken place since the 1870s view. One of the most significant changes was to turn the platform on the left into an island and give the formerly embayed track easy access to the turntable

Turning the platform into an island created a difficulty in how to provide access. This was resolved by provision of gangplank bridges between the platfoms, one of which is clearly in use in this picture of the station taken about 1914. To the left of the island platform is the locomotive *Ventnor* of the IOWR, which became No. W15 *Ventnor* after Grouping.

Ventnor Station, September 1952.

No. W17 *Seaview* emerges from the tunnel.

In the photographs above and below locomotive No. W26 *Whitwell* is being prepared for the return journey to Ryde, September 1965. After being cleaned out and taking on water, the engine will be run around to the other end of the coaches for the trip.

Ventnor Station from the Down above the tunnel, September 1965.
No. W20 *Shanklin* waits at the end of a long line of carriages. On
the right hand side of the photograph are caves that were cut into
the rockface by local businesses to store goods at the station.

Brading to Bembridge

Passenger services	27 May 1882 – 21 September 1953
Distance	2.75 miles
Companies	Brading Harbour Improvement & Railway;
	Isle of Wight Railway; Southern Railway;
	British Railways

Closed stations	Opening date	Closing date
St Helen's	27 May 1882	21 September 1953
Bembridge	27 May 1882	21 September 1953

The town of Brading was once a major port on the island, however this changed when the Brading Harbour Improvement & Railway Company was set up by Jabez Balfour MP in 1874. The company received authorisation on 7 August that year to construct an embankment from St Helen's to Bembridge and to reclaim all the land upstream towards Brading, to construct a port at St Helen's, and finally to build a branch line from the Isle of Wight Railway at Brading to Bembridge, via St Helen's. This work, along with several other projects in the area, was financed by the Liberator Building Society and cost £420,000.

Brading to Bembridge was the only branch line on the Isle of Wight. The line left Brading via a junction facing Ventnor, ran over the reclaimed estuary lands and was practically level. At the terminus, Bembridge, there was a turntable, which allowed the engine to run round its train. The turntable measured 16 feet, 5 inches in length.

The railway company was the harbour authority in Bembridge and it also owned the toll road between St Helen's and Bembridge. The line opened on 27 May 1882, in time for the Whitsun holiday, when it was said that three hundred St Helen's and Brembridge villagers took advantage of a free trip to Ryde. The local press had largely ignored the construction of the line, so its opening received only a brief report in the Isle of Wight Times on Thursday, 1 June 1882. Between Brading and St Helen's there was a spur heading to a brick works which was built in 1880 and known as Carpenters of Faithfulls Siding.

On the final day a large number of villagers turned out to ride on the last train. Among these was Herbert Occomore who, for many years, was the harbour master and pilot at Bembridge. He had also travelled on the very first train from Brading to St Helen's in 1881.

St Helen's Station, September 1952.

From St Helen's a short line ran to a quay in Brading Harbour. Here a group of men pose with three wagons and a locomotive being delivered to the island. The date is probably 1898; the marking on the wagons look as if they are intended for the Isle of Wight Central Railway and the last engine with a matching wheel configuration was delivered to them in April that year.

In June 1913 these carriages were delivered to the island for the Freshwater, Yarmouth & Newport Railway.

A continuation of the events in the previous picture as the carriages are unloaded from the barge. The locomotive sandwiched between the carriages here would become *Freshwater*. The engine was the second of two that the Freshwater, Yarmouth and Newport Railway bought during the period that followed the collapse of the agreement with the Isle of Wight Central Railway and had to run their line with their own rolling stock. *Freshwater* was originally built in 1876 by the London, Brighton and South Coast Railway as No. 646 *Newington* before being sold to the London and South Western Railway in May 1903 as their No. 734. On the island the locomotive lasted well, receiving the No. W2 from the Southern Railway at the Grouping. It was eventually withdrawn from service by British Rail in November 1963.

A view from Bembridge over Brading Harbour with the railway in the foreground, *c.* 1910.

Ryde at Bembridge Station, *c.* 1914.

No. W13 *Ryde* at Bembridge Station, July 1928.

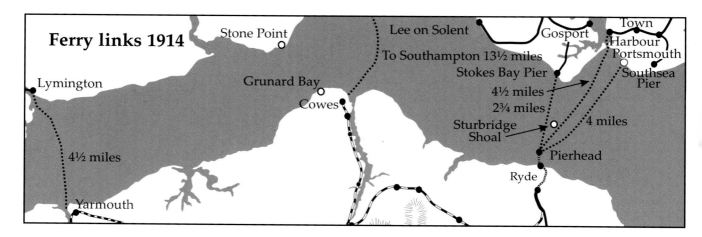

Ferry links 1914

Stone Point

Lee on Solent

Town

Gosport

Harbour

Portsmouth

To Southampton 13½ miles

Stokes Bay Pier

Southsea Pier

Lymington

Grunard Bay

Cowes

4½ miles

2¾ miles

Sturbridge Shoal

4 miles

4½ miles

Pierhead

Ryde

Yarmouth

Tunnel Visions

Almost as soon as railways were established on the Isle of Wight, the idea of a tunnel connecting the island with the mainland was suggested. In 1871 the engineer Charles Vignoles proposed a railway tunnel between Stone Point and Gurnard Bay and a number of test bores were made off Stone Point in 1874. The intention was to assess the practicality for a junction railway between the London & South Western Railway at Totton (near Southampton) and the island's developing railway network. The bores showed that clays underlay much of the Solent and encouraged interest in the project. The Midland & South Western Railway in particular considered the scheme to be important, and were latterly strongly associated with it, to the extent that they considered changing the name of the company to the Midland and Isle of Wight Railway. However, the line from Totton remained unbuilt, and even a reduced plan to build a railway pier at Stone Point failed to start, mainly as a result of objections from vested shipping interests, and the project petered out.

In 1886 a second scheme began to connect Ryde to Stokes Bay where the London and South Western Railway had built a pier in the 1870s. George Stulz Wells tried to encourage interest in a tunnel between the two points. He managed to interest the Admiralty who considered that a fort on Sturbridge Shoal in the Solent could be served by the proposed railway, making it virtually unassailable, and that it would also reduce the chance of the Isle of Wight being seized by an enemy power during a war. In spite of Wells's early success, neither government nor the railway companies were altogether impressed. After a disastrous public meeting in Ryde in October 1876 that nobody attended except Wells, the mayor and a few reporters, the project sank into obscurity.

A third attempt was made in 1901 when the South Western & Isle of Wight Junction Railway bill was heard in parliament. This proposal concerned the far west of the island. The railway would use the Lymington Branch of the London & South Western Railway on the mainland, tunnel under the Solent and come to the surface between Yarmouth and Freshwater. A continuation of the Freshwater, Yarmouth & Newport Railway's line from Freshwater to Totland Bay was included. Considerable opposition was made by the Isle of Wight Railway, who stood to lose most if a tunnel didn't connect directly to their network. The tunnel failed to materialise within the time limit for work to start, however several time extensions were made to the bill and it seemed more likely that this time the tunnel would be built. It was against that background that relationships between the Isle of Wight Central Railway and the Freshwater, Yarmouth & Newport Railway began to sour. This culminated in the termination of the joint running agreement between the two companies in 1913. In spite of having been essentially bankrupt the FY&NR managed overnight to become the smartest looking line on the island. Stations were refurbished, well upholstered carriages were purchased, and two locomotives shipped to the island. The locomotives were painted in a fresh green livery that reminded most observers of the mainland's Great Central Railway and prompted a great deal of rumour that the line had been bought by that company. Certainly the GCR had shown interest in the project but no direct connection between it and the FY&NR can be made, and it isn't clear how the transformation was achieved. The start of the First World War in August 1914 ends the story of the company's metamophosis and the prospect of the tunnel.

Between the First and Second World Wars there was considerable activism to try to interest the railway companies and others to construct a tunnel to the mainland but against a background of wartime reconstruction and recession no project was seriously considered.

Since the Second World War several proposals have been made, the majority of which have been road tunnels. However, two of the most recent , in 2002 and 2008, were for a rail or light rail tunnel. However, public opinion on the island has shifted significantly and both proposals were fiercely opposed by the residents.